Atlas Apothecary

poems by

Tom Plante

Finishing Line Press
Georgetown, Kentucky

Atlas Apothecary

ACKNOWLEDGMENTS

Poems in this book have appeared (sometimes in earlier versions) in the
following anthologies and magazines:
The Art of Survival: An Anthology (Kings Estate Press)
At the Gate: Arrivals and Departures (Kings Estate Press)
The Carriage House Poetry Series 10th Anniversary Anthology (Muse-Pie Press)
Contrarywise: An Anthology (Kings Estate Press)
Edison Literary Review
Exit 13 Magazine
Home Planet News
Lips Magazine
Tiferet Journal

Editor: Christen Kincaid

Cover Art: Compass Rose, Shutterstock.com

Author Photo: Patricia Plante

Cover Design: Elizabeth Maines

Printed in the USA on acid-free paper.
Order online: www.finishinglinepress.com
            also available on amazon.com

Author inquiries and mail orders:
Finishing Line Press
P. O. Box 1626
Georgetown, Kentucky 40324
U. S. A.

Table of Contents

*For my wife, Patricia; our daughter, Kerry Marie;
and our families – Love Always.*

LOVE AT WORK
– for Trish

Sitting at my typewriter
with an hour to go
I jump the tracks
in a desperate urge
to see you sooner
cut across the field
golden with summer
grass thigh high
hurdle a low fence
clear another yard
dart between cars
and head for your block.

But the clock crawls
and let's face it
you're three thousand
some odd miles away
home already in another
time zone, your shoes
off, fans on.
All the shortcuts
in the world won't
get me there faster.
As I kiss you
my elbow hits RETURN.

ATLAS APOTHECARY

Where did I put the geography
the wholeness of this place?
Each piece compartmentalized:
air direction velocity humor
feathers oils ribs groins
top shelf farther left
up above the plateau
beyond the sink hole
meadow moraine
where sand grains loiter
seeds fall and wait for rain
back wall near the window
where mornings are kept
alphabetical by month
miles from here on maps
rolled under beds
near closets of cotton
and woolen wharves asleep
by restless rivers running past
igneous ridges and crystalline
columns near the corner
by the bank
where the post office stood
before BlackBerrys.

UNFINISHED WORK

for Stuart B. Plante and Allen Ginsberg

Unexpected April snow precedes another passing.
The spring we long for waits another day.
Unfinished work gets one more glance indoors,
another chance to sort and tinker
though there'll always be unfinished work.
The snow itself interferes but twice
in 15 years the spring event meant
a wise grey man would leave us with the melt:
first my father in '82 and now the famous poet.

"If you're not careful you'll wind up like Allen Ginsberg,"
my father once shouted as I left the house
for a gig with some high school musicians.
Dad didn't care for the beads around my neck
and probably wouldn't care for my version
of "House of the Rising Sun" either.

There is still birdsong through spring's open window
and crabs search for their new shells.
Onion grass and forsythia burst the dull landscape
as cherry blossoms dare to be fragile despite
the chance of plummeting temperatures overnight.

The roses sprout leaves and new thorns.
Lilies push mud aside. Slowly the pain of growth
and loss gives way to full bloom and fruit,
sunflowers and summer's abundant gardens.
But the memory of the last storm still lingers.
April will get a second chance to signal new life.
But it will have to wait a day until another
grey head rests beneath the sod
and shovels return to other tasks
to take up other useful jobs.

PROPAGANDA

I sit in my office writing propaganda.
I grow the best tomatoes in the world.
My string beans have been better
but what the heck, they're fresh
and they run up the trellis like the rest
spinning and swirling and looping
through available space to grab
hold or wrap around something stable
substantial, a pole or wire or
plant stem that hardens.
The lettuce is buttery except for the
arugula, the bite of earth in every
leaf and stem. Where did I get
those seeds? Maybe I could go into
the arugula business, corner the market.
My dad said don't do for a living
what you love to do. He was an
appraiser and office manager by day,
a master carpenter at home by night.
Guess which paid the mortgage and
put four kids through school.
And he grew rhubarb, the best in the world.

CICADA LATER

– Fanwood, New Jersey 1996

In 17 years I'll be 64
and the cicadas
won't remember me
reincarnated as they'll be
kids really, they won't remember
my leaf blower pushing
their parents down the
driveway into the street.

It wasn't me, it was
neighborhood cars ran them over
too late to do any good.
The eggs only heard the
whirring we all heard
the air thick with sound
from big winged bugs that
cling to trees and come up
from the ground.

In 17 years I may
not hear them again
or care what the crunch
under foot is. I may even
welcome those old buggers.

THE PLAN FOR TODAY

My Saturday coffee is lukewarm
but there are three ripe blueberries this morning.
I'll take the good with the bad.

My love dashed away early
but the rabbits haven't eaten our lettuce.
The day promises to be bright and sweaty.

The lessons of the morning
are strewn throughout the house,
their subtlety piled for later celebration.

The goldfinches are interrupted
by my 12-year-old's call.
We'll rendezvous at the stable.

Where has the sun of dawn
journeyed to now that it's 10 a.m.?
Somewhere a symphony is tuning up for another show.

My songs return from another century;
their smiles are worn but their grip is strong.
Between them the cicadas applaud.

My love will return home before evening;
our daughter will stay with friends.
I'll sing to them from the steps.

UNPLUGGED MELODY

I'm mostly unplugged these days
though I understand the value of amplification.
My dad used to say he could
hear me down the block.

I can't tell Nirvana from Maroon 5
but I hear the cardinals singing in the hedges
and I can differentiate
the Animals from the Stones.

I've learned from the mockingbird
and the woodpecker
about imitation and persistence,
though I was told once
by a friend in confidence
that I was no Ella Fitzgerald.

FERRY 'CROSS THE DELAWARE

The Delaware yawns
as we cross her mouth
wider than our eyes,
the ferry packed with
tongues from other lands.
We're back from the Outer Banks
and headed to Cape May –
our New Jersey bobs in the waves.
We sail through the pitch,
a bit of sea and bay,
our sea legs recalled
and our neighborly ways –
snapping pictures with a
salmon sunset background:
the white and brown skin,
some East Europeans and Asians,
Latinos, tall, short, stout,
shorts, sandals, kids and
lovers of all shapes,
fingers entwined, teens
shying from parental hugs,
plowing the mouth of
this great river, severing
time and place, a raft
afloat in sea saltiness
and the fresh water flowing
down from the mountains
of New York, Pennsylvania
and the Garden State,

flowing across our path
as we share the rail
with the wide-eyed, lovers
and families making the voyage,
crossing the mouth together.

GLOBAL

The salesman's English
is pretty poor
but he sold ten cars
this week, he smiled.

His wife and child
live in Colombia.
Manny's been too busy
to learn the language.

In three or six months
his boy will come
but not the mom.
She's not ready.

Her forms were rejected.
You like the car, Mr. Tom?
he manages as other
customers wait.

Here's a picture, he hands
me his cell phone
with a little boy on the screen,
the son he's never seen.

CORAL AVENUE MORNING, 8-31-05

Just the wind and the sun
to greet me this morning,
the sound of air flowing
through white oaks,
leaves like fingers
playing natural notes.
Just the crape myrtles in bloom
in brilliant white and berry shades.
Just the monarchs fleeing south
from one butterfly bush to another
down quiet streets hushed to hear
the news of the surf from over the dunes.
Just the love songs of cicadas
from trees and shrubs at the Point.
Just the hawks and falcons fattening
in the marsh for their flight
to a warmer climate south of here.
Just the begonias' shadows
and the undersides of leaves
trading faces with the breeze.
Just another day for sand dune meandering
up and down the seaboard,
rolling and tumbling to the tide's tune,
shifting the furnishings one more time.
Just a day for a fat-tire bike ride
to gather a forecast,
check the dragon flies and
the stature of gnarled pines,
catch the sun as it shines

and breathe the peace between
fronts and backyard fences
ahead of the worst storm of our time
as news of Hurricane Katrina
breaks along the Jersey Shore.

HOTEL RUMINATIONS IN SAN FRANCISCO

Waiting for you at the St. Francis
down the street from that other
Francis, Drake the pirate.
What's the difference?
One fed the birds,
the other fed the sharks.
We make our own memories.
I'm still carving my niche
on this pad with small pages.
My bad thumb holds the page still.
The good one holds the pen
that corrals me so you'll find
just what you'd expect when you
return: scratchy surprises
on a leaf blowing uphill.

ASPHALT GEOGRAPHY

At the corner of West First and Amsterdam
the perfume is French from Port-au-Prince,
cumulous T-shirts billowing white
from the Welsh Farms store
are reminders that here, at the crossroads
of all we know, the journey is ongoing,
the slow wait and the sudden turn together
in our home for the moment, our refuge,
a birthplace for some on life's terrain
wedged within the left turn lane
and the Jersey Transit trestle,
the Victory Box lot
and the corner bus stop.

Life drives others here, to take flight
in apartments above the Egg Factory
and on stoops in neat fenced yards
while cars of every shape and color,
make and model, prepare to drive away.

Little Jimmy's Italian Ices
sit in a driveway waiting for summer,
waiting to play "Home, Home on the Range"
over and over again
through neighborhoods of childhood games.
Others await repairs on blocks, rims
rusty for a time but ready someday
to return to the roads between the rivers.

To the east is the Hudson,
to the west the Delaware,
closer yet the Rahway and the Elizabeth.

At this concrete confluence of busy streets
there is time for reflection.
The corner of West First and Amsterdam
is like many others
where brothers and sisters
move with their own current
as time and transit stand still.

Someone will run a light.
Someone will jaywalk in a fog.
There's a sound that tires make
rubbing the road the wrong way,
a note or two of cacophony,
Bluebirds belching diesel, shifting gears
at the school bus yard nearby.

This isn't Swansea or the Champs-Elysees,
just a pocket of peace
in a concrete concerto –
two tributaries form a "T"
in a land the glaciers left behind
in the space between two rivers.

FREE SHOW

World War II bombers
lumber through the late
August afternoon, practicing
for an air show
in Wildwood over
Labor Day weekend.
The year is 2007.

A young boy next door to
our cottage at the Point
ignores history's props
and hoses down his
swim trunks, his bare
white butt as free as the
gulls combing the beach.

THE ASSIGNMENT

The book review is due in a few days.
A basket of socks rests on the bed in front of me.
It's an anthology with dozens of poems.
A cold beer waits for me on the night stand.
Humidity tightens my t-shirt.
The grey sky has a fringe of thunder.
August swirls in the window fans.
The dry yard is dotted with tomatoes.
A goldfinch stops by for thistle seeds
unmoved by a barking dog.

I like the book and the beer,
honeysuckle and the Rose of Sharon,
the goldfinch and tomatoes.
Rain is expected on the pages of poems
when I get them outside with my shirt off,
barefoot with delight, riding their crests
after I sort the socks.

IN CASE

Bring your jacket
just in case the forest
trail is damp and cool.
You can always take it off
when the morning ride
turns warm in the clearing,
clouds shedding their coats
to run in every direction,
beams of light streaking
to the soft dust under hoof.

Bring your crop just in case.
You can slip it on your wrist
and walk on. The calm can be
deceiving, buttercups distracting.
You never know what your horse
sees in the shadows or what the
hawks are doing. What matters
is that you're ready for whatever,
as if you could be
ready for anything.

TOO MANY SERGEANTS
10-17-06

A lot of sergeants make the list
of those killed in Iraq fighting terror –
sergeants from Iowa City, Portland,
Cedar Grove and a thousand other
peaceful towns that dot the landscape
of these United States. Their names
are broadcast in silence on the evening news
as photographs become available. Each
gets a few seconds of remembrance at
the end of the News Hour on PBS.
Invariably I stop chopping vegetables
to note their age, home town, and rank –
a last look at their eyes.
Too young, too old, too many.
And so many sergeants, servants
of our country who worked their way
up the ranks. So many towns with
rural roots and even the cities more
pastoral, peaceful, than far-off Iraq
and forgotten Afghanistan, our wars
of choice that offer brief geography lessons
to a people struggling to understand our kids,
our computers, our insurance policies, iPods,
new fangled contraptions and the grains of
sand that take our sons and daughters
through the hourglass of our times,
the niece's husband back from the
first assault on Saddam, the nephew
now in Ramadi. The names and places
embedded out of sight.

GREETINGS FROM IRAQ
– for Sgt. Andy Dinsmore
2-7-07

Don't rest the pizza box
on Andy's postcard from Iraq.
Sauce from the pie might
mess up his message.

He reminds us what's important –
How is school? The weather?
It's been cold here and rainy,
he writes from the desert.

We'll start another family letter
after we finish the pie.
I'm still good, he says.
Just wanted to say hi.

Every word is thoughtful
from the boy who has grown.
Ready to go back to Ramadi.
Only two months and I'm home.

TUNE IN TOMORROW FOR ANOTHER ADVENTURE

When my brother and I were younger
we read Superman comic books and
watched his adventures on TV.
Our Uncle Gene worked for Philco
and we had the only TV set on our block.
We sent away for Superman t-shirts
and when they arrived at our house
my brother and I were thrilled.
Of course that was more than 50 years ago
and neither of us really expected Superman
to crash to earth as a baby from Krypton
and be raised by Ma and Pa Kent.
But in today's news there's a story
about a privately owned jet plane rocket
that blasted out of earth's atmosphere and
later returned safely to earth with its passengers.
And another about four more Americans
killed in Iraq. There were probably
Americans stationed in harm's way the day
our Superman t-shirts arrived back in the 1950s.
But we were brave adventurous boys who
paid no attention to world news. We knew the
dangers of kryptonite and Lex Luther and the limits
of X-ray vision but knew next to nothing
about the hazards of the DMZ in Korea
or the Berlin wall, what the heck was Indo-China
or what was going on along the back roads of Alabama.
Superman's rocket crashed near a small
out-of-the-way town long before they made
a television series about it called Smallville.

I haven't seen the show about Clark's juvenile days
probably because I watch so much TV news
and am fascinated now by adventures
of a different sort and other far-flung places
like the Khyber Pass, the Isles of
Langerhans and the Strait of Hormuz.

LOOKING FOR IT ON THE OUTER BANKS

Spent the better part of the day
looking for it, its parts like a gear
smooth when assembled,
knowing each fraction of it rests
somewhere I've been,
so now I retrace my steps,
over dunes, down stairs
shouldered with sea oats
to sandy thresholds
greeted by sanderlings and
brown pelicans nose diving.

Looking for it at waves edge
that moves with the moon,
the Gulf Stream and the
fickle crabs fleeing from sight.

Step by step with the rising tide,
in sync with the gulls who wish me gone,
I keep looking for it, glasses fogged
with the mist chance of a storm,
then witness the ascension of kites
as their ragged tails salute
the wind's teeth.

FORAGING IN WESTFIELD

Circling the lot
at Trader Joe's
and finally finding
a parking spot, I realize
it's reserved for
Wachovia customers.

I take a chance
on being towed
and head for the store
wanting only blueberries
but notice a hawk
circling low over the lot.

Entering the market
I observe the express
line, twenty deep.
Frozen blueberries can wait.
I retreat to the lot,
hawk gone, car untowed.

FOR THE SOULS OF THE LOWER 9th WARD

Hurricane Katrina bent down
and kissed the belt
around the Crescent City.
The levees held
along the Mississippi
protecting shivering shacks
and modest mansions
but the storm surge
from Lake Pontchartrain
and the Industrial Canal
broke the belt
and blew in the backdoor
to level the score
raising the lowest
off the first floor
and through the roof
leaving generations lost
and ruined homes
unattended for weeks.
Now grassy plots obscure
historic homelands
of former slaves and freedmen
musicians and custodians
their family trees uprooted
by surging water
Neptune ordered.
The only clues to their owners'
whereabouts are the stone
front stairs to nowhere.

When keyboards rattle
and clarinets cry
remember the souls
of the Lower 9th Ward
as you look to the sky
and hear them at your door.

ON MAGAZINE STREET, NEW ORLEANS

On the shady side
of Magazine, I rest
digest alligator sausage
with Abita Springs beer
served Camp Street style,
my head stuffed with
days and nights
of Vieux Carre rhythms
on the Bourbon Street bayou,
ready to burst with good times
yet saddened by rotted porches
and door frames where
the lost took refuge
and the present find work.

Amazed by all the traffic
on Magazine and along
the bright Mississippi
that doesn't stop, just slows
to let souls cross
from one side to another,
I sit, my brown beer bag
a membrane between
bad days and better,
and recall hopeful assurance
hand painted on a wall:
We'll be back, come
Hell or high water.

MORNING IN THE QUARTER
(New Orleans, 2009)

On the morning of
my 60th birthday
I crossed Chartres Street
to buy a cup of milk.

The sidewalk in front
of Sneaky Pete's
was bleached. The Harem
ladies were home asleep.

I got milk and The Times-
Picayune and returned
to our brick-walled room
to enjoy Community Coffee.

Workmen in overalls were up
early, drilling and sanding
the hotel doors, loudly
proclaiming the break of dawn.

Sixty years to the day,
I celebrate the noise and humidity,
await a cab to Louis Armstrong Airport
for our flight to New Jersey,

happy to be in the Crescent City,
young at heart in the Vieux Carre,
not crazy about leaving,
still ready to dance the day away.

LUCKY BONES

I toast the soft wheat
Pepperidge Farm bread

with a cup of Morning Blend
and a Cricket Hill Pale Ale

toast my lucky bones
and the whispering house

spared the slap of yesterday's
tropical storm-force wind

toast the postal worker's
song-drenched delivery

and the Brooklyn poems
that sailed to New Jersey

toast the Saturday chores
after Friday night laughter

phone calls in pajamas
and dinner plans with friends

toast Valentine's kisses
sweet through the stitches.

44th & OCEAN, BRANT BEACH, NJ

The early risers know them:
garage sale skimmers on quiet streets,
beach combers and shell seekers,
surf casters in the first
salty rays of dawn.

Some say there's nothing there,
just someone else's junk;
the morning haul of
treasure by a curbside or
that perfect scalloped shell,
only a gifted scavenger can tell.

It's all there: sparkles
inching closer to shore,
inspiration at your fingertips,
the day's catch waiting
for a studied hand,
and me on the tide's edge
keeping record in the sand.

AUTUMN SERENADE IN DUCK, NC

*"Even a grey day
is a good day now."*
— *Tom Paxton*

The mockingbirds are back
cheerfully ridiculing the forecasters
in their suits and ties who predict
a 30 percent chance of rain, a slight
improvement over yesterday's 40 percent.
A lone pelican glides the length
of a long roller gracefully
forgetting the tumultuous sea so
inhospitable just hours ago.
The elders who witness these natural
rhythms of sea and sky discerning
slight variations in shade and hue,
fret occasionally but remind
one another it's better than a good
day in a cubicle, brighten with
songs of their own, ballads of
boyhood and backseat tales,
their offspring back in school
or grandkids pestering their own
generation beyond the tumbling
of the tides and the outlook
for tomorrow, the chance of sun
and rugged nesters awakening
in the brambles by the sea oats,
golden rod, crab apples and
wild roses. Somewhere we all
found shelter in the teeming
storm; now the songs form.

Tom Plante was born in New York City and grew up in East Rockaway. His first real job was delivering Newsday while in grammar school. While he was earning a B.A. in Geography from the University of California at Berkeley, he was a writer for the *Berkeley Barb* and participated in poetry readings throughout the San Francisco Bay Area. Tom published a poetry magazine, *Berkeley Works* (1981-85), and labored in the wholesale book business before moving to New Jersey in 1986. His newspaper work continued with stints at the *Irish Echo* in New York City and the *Scotch Plains-Fanwood Times*, and finally with ten years at the *Courier-News* in Bridgewater, NJ. In 1996, he was awarded a first prize for editorial writing by the New Jersey Press Association.

Since 1988, Tom Plante has edited *EXIT 13 Magazine*, an annual journal of poetry with a geographic focus. (www.facebook.com/ Exit13Magazine). Previous collections of his poetry include *Wear and Tear* (Crosscut Saw Publications) and *My Back Yardstick* (CC Marimbo). His writing has appeared in the *Berkeley Poetry Review, Second Coming, Beatitude, Love Lights, City Miner, Edison Literary Review, Lips Magazine, Home Planet News, Journal of New Jersey Poets, Tiferet Journal, Small Press Review, Northeast Rising Sun, Ireland of the Welcomes*, and other periodicals and anthologies. Tom works for the County of Union NJ, and lives in Fanwood, New Jersey with his wife and daughter.

www.ingramcontent.com/pod-product-compliance
Lightning Source LLC
LaVergne TN
LVHW090015090426
835509LV00035BA/1270